The Touch of Gold
and other stories

Adapted by Sheila Lane and Marion Kemp

Illustrations by Roger Waites

Take Part Starters

Level 3

W **Ward Lock Educational Co. Ltd.**

Ward Lock Educational Co. Ltd.
BIC Ling Kee House
1 Christopher Road
East Grinstead
Sussex RH19 3BT

A member of the Ling Kee Group
London · Hong Kong · New York · Singapore

© Sheila Lane and Marion Kemp
This edition published 1991
ISBN 0 7062 5160 1

Reprinted 1997

Printed in Hong Kong

Contents

1 The Touch of Gold   4

2 The Bag of Winds   14

3 The King's New Clothes   26

★ This sign means that
you can make the sounds
which go with the story.

The Touch of Gold

This is Midas, a Greek King.

This is his daughter, the Princess.

This is a Wise Man.

This is the Servant.

King Midas is sitting on the throne in his palace.

King Midas How happy I am! Today I am the happiest man in the world.

Wise Man What has made you so happy, O King?

King Midas I have been given a wish. It is a gift from the gods.

Servant What did you wish for, O King?

King Midas I wished for a magic power.

Servant What can it do, O King?

King Midas It can turn all things to gold. By the touch of my hand, I can turn all things to gold.

Wise Man So you have The Touch of Gold!

King Midas I can make myself the richest man in the world.

Wise Man But can you make yourself happy?

King Midas Gold will bring happiness. Gold is the best and most wonderful thing in the world. I will show my magic power to my daughter, the Princess.

Servant She is not here, O King.

Wise Man   Your daughter is out in the palace garden.

King Midas   Then let us go out into the garden . . .
Daughter! Daughter!

Princess   I am here, father.

Wise Man   Your father has a magic power, O princess.

Princess   What is that?

Servant   The King can make gold.

Princess   How can he do that?
Show me how to make gold, father.

King Midas   You will soon see, my dear. Bring me a flower
and I will turn it to gold.

Princess   Here is a red flower.

Servant   Now the red flower is turned to gold!

Princess   Here is a blue flower.

Servant   Now the blue flower is turned to gold.

King Midas This is wonderful! I will touch all the flowers in the garden.

Wise Man You can have a garden full of gold flowers, O King. But can you make yourself happy?

King Midas Gold will bring happiness. Gold is the best and most wonderful thing in the world.

Princess Father! Put your hand on a tree.
Show us how to make a gold tree.

Servant Make a tree of gold, O King.

King Midas There you are! That is wonderful!
I can have trees with beautiful golden apples
and beautiful golden . . .

Wise Man You can have trees of gold in your garden, O King.
But can you make yourself happy?

King Midas Gold will bring happiness. I am the happiest man
in the world. Bring me food and wine,
so that I can be merry.

Servant Here is the food and wine, O King.

Princess O father! You have put your hand on the food
and it has turned to gold.

Servant The cup and the wine have turned to gold too.

King Midas   Now that I have The Touch of Gold, I cannot use my hands when I want to eat or drink. What shall I do?

Princess   Father! I will help you.
Let me give you . . .

Wise Man   No! Do not touch the Princess, O King! Oh! Oh! It is too late . . .

Servant   Too late! The King has put his hand on the Princess.

King Midas What shall I do? What have I done?
My lovely daughter is a cold, gold statue.

Wise Man Will your golden child bring you happiness now,
O King?

Servant What can the King do now?

King Midas I have lost my child.
I have lost the one I loved best in the world.

Wise Man You said that gold would bring you happiness.
Now you know that this is not so.

King Midas Who will take this magic power from me?
Who will take away this Touch of Gold?

Wise Man A gift from the gods must be given back
to the gods.

Servant How can this be?

Wise Man It can be washed away by the waters of the sea
and sent back to the place from which it came.

King Midas Let me give it back to the gods. Let me go down
to the sea and wash away my gift.

Wise Man   This you can do, O King. Go down to the seashore
If you really wish to lose The Touch of Gold,
it can be washed away by the waters of the sea.

The King did as the Wise Man said and from that day to this the sands of the sea have been a golden colour.

Things for you to do

1 | g) o l d | ends with) o l d .

Use these letters and write more words which end with) o l d .

b)   c)   f)   h)   s)   t

2 Write each sentence with the right word from the story.

(a) King Midas could turn all things to (silver/gold).

(b) King Midas said that gold would bring (happiness/sadness).

(c) The princess was in the palace (garden/tower).

(d) When the Touch of Gold was washed away the sand became a (golden/red) colour.

3 Write these sentences in the right order for the story.

Next he touched a tree.
First King Midas touched the flowers.
Then he touched his food and wine.

4 This is King Midas.
saying the lines from his
part.

By the touch of my hand I can turn all things to gold.

Who said these lines?

(a) But can you make yourself happy?
(b) Here is the food and wine, O King.
(c) Father, I will help you.

Draw the pictures and write the words.

The Bag of Winds

This is the King.

This is the Captain of the Ship.

This is Jason.

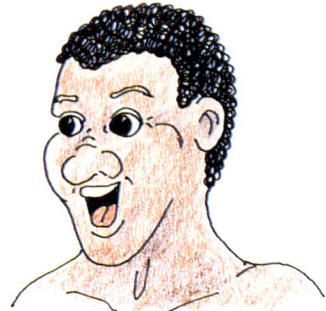

This is Ajax.

They are the Captain's men.

Many years ago, the King set out on a voyage to his island home across the sea.

Captain We have a good west wind, O King. Soon we shall see the shores of your island home.

King It is ten long years since I saw my island home.

Captain Run the sails up, Ajax. You too, Jason.
Run the sails up.

Ajax   I will do it, Captain.

Jason   And I.

King   How long will it be before I see my island home again?

Captain   It will not be long. The sails are full of wind already. Ho there, Ajax!

Ajax   Ho there, Captain!

Captain   Ho there, Jason!

Jason   Ho there, Captain!

Captain   You are tired, O King. Let us go down below where you can rest for the voyage.

King   I cannot rest. After so many years I cannot rest until I see my island home again.

Captain   I can promise that the voyage will not be long. This good west wind will carry us fair and true.

Ajax   Ho there, Captain!
The sails are set.

Jason Ho there, Captain!
The wind is good.

Captain It seems as if this west wind knows of your wish
to hurry home, O King.

King That is so.

Captain You speak as if you had some secret power
over the winds, O King.

King Perhaps I have.
The good west wind blows fair and true.
This I can promise all of you.

Ajax How can you do that, O King?

Jason Are you the King of the Winds?

King No, I am King of the island
which is my home across the sea.
But this I promise all of you.
This wind will blow us fair and true.

Captain If you will not go down below,
perhaps you will rest here on the deck?

King I will do that. I will rest on the deck so that I can keep a look-out for the shore of my island home.

Ajax I will take your bag, O King.

King No! Take your hand away.

Jason Let me.

King No, I say! Keep off!

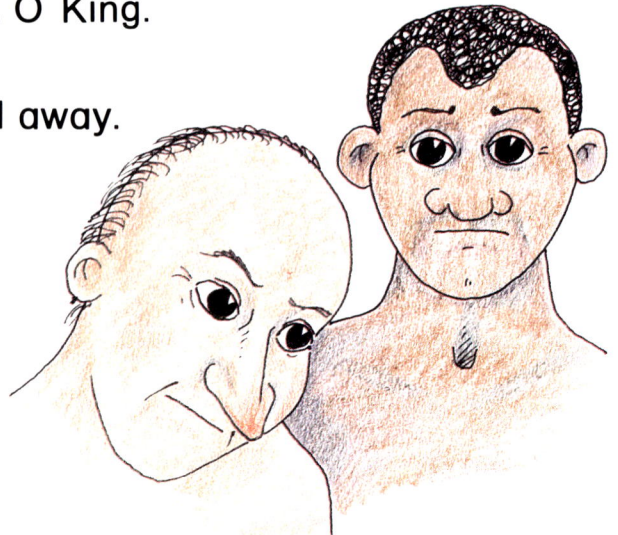

Captain Then take your leather bag in your own hand and let it rest beside you.

King I will do that. I will rest here and keep a look-out over the sea until I see my island home again.

Captain Come over here, men. Let the King rest. After ten long years he thinks of nothing but his home.

Ajax We will let him rest.

Jason Ten years away from home is a long time.

Captain I wonder if his family and friends will remember him after so long a time.

Ajax They will remember.

Jason Yes, Captain.
They will remember.

Captain How can you be so sure?

Ajax He has a bag of gold.

Jason They will want his gold.

Captain How can you be so sure that the bag is full of gold?

Ajax Look at his hand.

Jason His hand is on the bag.
It MUST be gold.

Captain This King is a strange man. They say that he is a
great hero. They say that he has killed many men.

Jason Look! He is asleep.

Ajax His bag is by his side.

Jason But look!
His hand is not on the bag.

Ajax Captain! Let us . . .

Captain I know what is in your mind. But . . .
This King paid us well for the voyage.

Jason He did not give us gold from his bag.

Captain Wait! The bag is made of leather and is tied
with a silver cord. Perhaps . . . Perhaps . . .

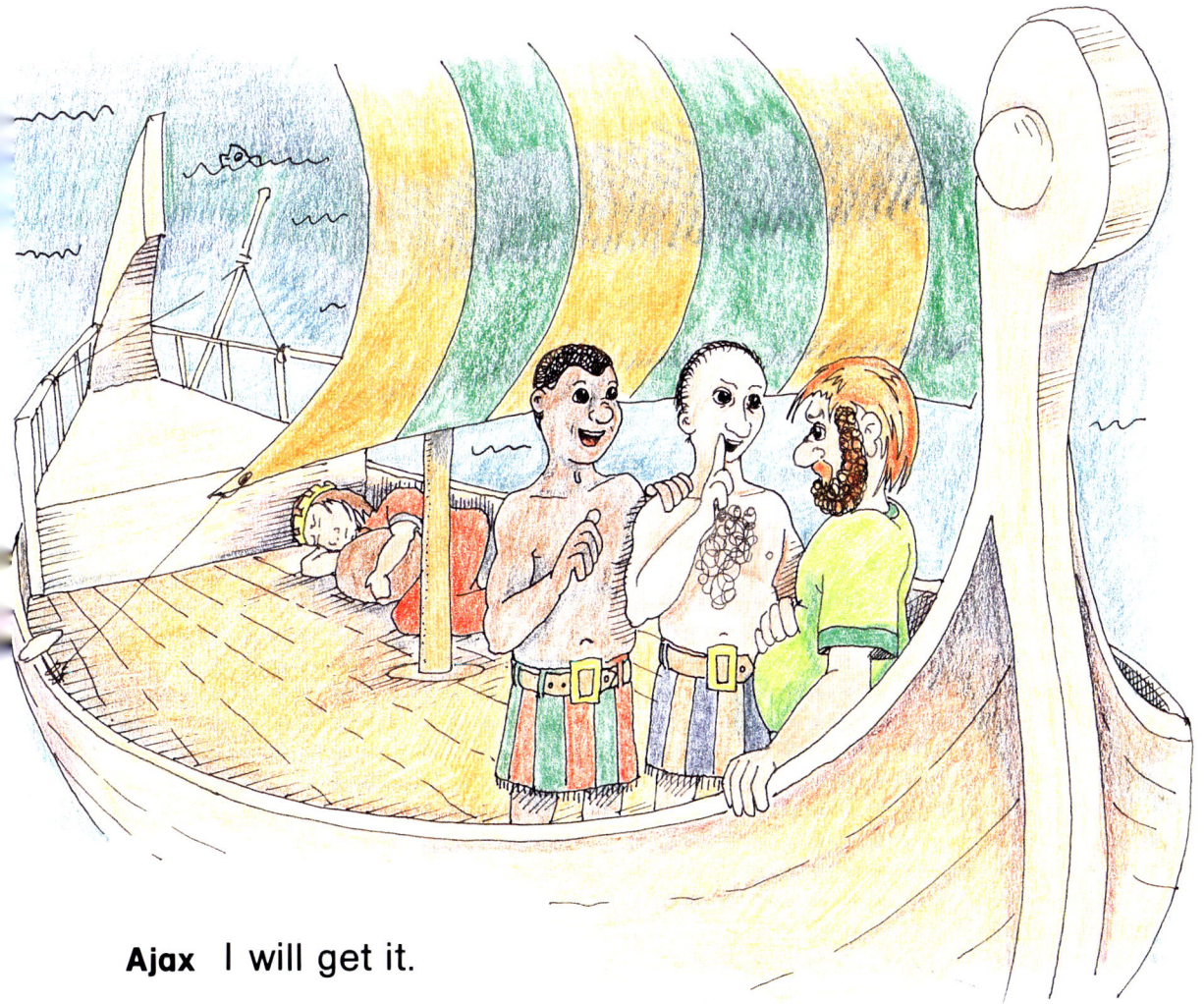

Ajax   I will get it.

Jason   No, me.

Captain You fools! If you call out like that, the King will
             wake up. You must creep towards him quietly.

Ajax   You go this time, Jason.

Captain No! Wait! The King is moving in his sleep . . .
             Now, Jason . . . Go!

Ajax   He has it!
Jason has the bag!

Captain   Sh! Bring it over here and we will see what treasure
is inside. Is it heavy?

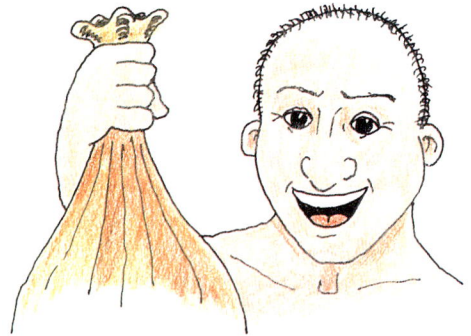

Jason   No, it is not heavy.

Ajax   Let me try it.
No, it is not heavy at all.

Captain   This is strange. The bag seems full and yet it is as
light as air. We will untie the silver cord together.
Take one end, Jason. Ajax! Take the other. Now . . .
PULL! ★

Ajax   What was that?

Captain   I felt a sudden rush of air like a mighty wind.

Jason   And so did I.

Ajax   But look!

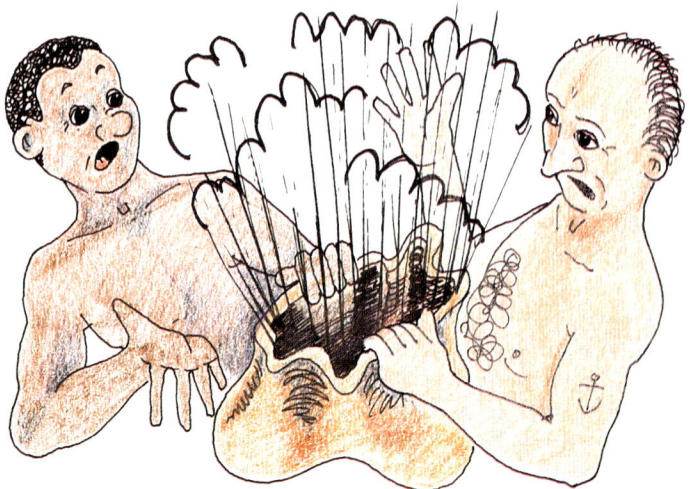

Jason   There is nothing in the bag.

Captain   The ship! The ship! The ship is turning like a top.

King   Captain! Captain! What is happening to the ship?

Captain   There is a great storm, O King. We have lost the good west wind which was blowing us towards your island home. The ship has turned round.

King   WHERE IS MY BAG?

Ajax   It is here.

King It's OPEN! You fools! Do you know what you have done?

Ajax We took no gold.

Jason There was no gold to take.

King You fools! You have opened the bag. You have let out the storm winds which were inside.

Captain STORM WINDS! So that is why you guarded the bag so carefully. And now the storm winds are blowing us AWAY from your island home, O King.

King Back, back, back across the sea,
Away from the home where I long to be.

Many, many years later, the King did reach his island home and he saw his wife and son again.

Things for you to do

1 s)a i l ends with)a i l .

Use these letters and make more words which end with)a i l .

m)   p)   t)   h)   w)   tr)

2 Write each sentence with the right word from the story.

(a) The King set out on a voyage to his island (castle/home).

(b) At first the good (west/north) wind blew fair and true.

(c) The King's (hand/head) was on the bag.

(d) The bag was tied with a (silver/gold) cord.

3 Write these sentences in the right order for the story.

Next there was a sudden rush of air like a mighty wind.
Then the ship began to turn like a top.
First Jason and Ajax pulled the cord from the bag.

4 This is the King
saying one of the lines
from his part.

It is ten long years since I saw my island home.

Who said these lines?

(a) I will take your bag, O King.
(b) There is nothing in the bag.
(c) I felt a sudden rush of air like a mighty wind.

Draw the pictures and write the words.

The King's New Clothes

This is the King.

This is the King's Servant.

This is the First Weaver.

This is the Second Weaver.

The two weavers are at the door of the great palace.

First Weaver This is the great palace where the King lives.
Now remember what we are going to say.

Second Weaver We are going to say . . .
We . . . are . . . going . . . to . . . say . . .

First Weaver There! You have forgotten already. We are
going to say that we will weave the most
beautiful clothes in the world for the King.

Second Weaver But . . . how . . . can . . . we . . . ?
I don't think we can do it.

First Weaver Just leave the thinking to me and
say what I say.
Now, knock on the door. ★

Second Weaver Sh! I can hear someone coming. ★

Servant Who are you? And what do you want?

First Weaver We are weavers, your Majesty.

Servant I am not the King. I am only his servant. You say you are weavers. The King has seen many weavers. Why should he want to see you? You will be no different from all the others.

First Weaver But we *are* different from other weavers. Our cloth is the most beautiful in the world. We have a magic touch.

Second Weaver   Yes, we have a magic touch.
The King will like our cloth.

Servant   The King loves beautiful clothes,
so I will ask him to see you. Come along.

First Weaver   This is a very fine palace.

Servant My King is the richest man in the world.
He only has the best of everything.
I will go and knock on the door
of the throne room. Wait here.

Second Weaver Do you think that the King will see us?

First Weaver Of course he will see us. Didn't I tell his
servant that we can weave the most beautiful
cloth in the world?

Second Weaver But . . . how . . . can . . . we . . . ?
I don't think we can do it.

First Weaver Just leave the thinking to me and say what I
say. This King loves fine clothes. People say
that he changes his clothes six times a day.
When we tell him that . . .

Second Weaver Sh! I can hear someone coming. ★

First Weaver It is only the Servant.
Now, my man, what did the King say?

Servant You may enter. The King will see you.

First Weaver Good morning, your Majesty.

Second Weaver Good morning, your Majesty.

King Good morning to you.

Servant These are the weavers I spoke of,
your Majesty.

First Weaver We have heard that you are looking for
weavers to make you the most beautiful suit
of clothes in the world.

Second Weaver We can do that, your Majesty.

King Tell me about it.

First Weaver The cloth we weave is the most beautiful in the world.

Second Weaver We have a magic touch, your Majesty.

Servant All weavers say that their cloth is better than anyone else's. Tell us why you think that yours is different.

King Tell us why your cloth is different.

First Weaver Our cloth can only be seen by those who are clever and wise.

Second Weaver You have to be wise or you cannot see it at all.

First Weaver People who are dull or stupid or not fit to do their jobs can't see the cloth at all.

Second Weaver They cannot see the cloth at all, your Majesty.

Servant Do you mean that this cloth is INVISIBLE?
Do you really mean that it can only be seen
by those who are clever and wise?

First Weaver Yes, it is invisible to all others.

Second Weaver Yes, it is invisible!

King INVISIBLE!

Servant This is most interesting. Your Majesty, if these
weavers make you some cloth, you will have a
fine suit of clothes AND you will also be able
to find out who is clever and who is stupid.

King I must have the clothes at once.

First Weaver Your Majesty . . . There is something else.

King Well, what is it?

First Weaver Our cloth is expensive. We have to be paid a
thousand gold pieces before we can begin
to work.

Second Weaver Yes, your Majesty. We cannot begin until we
have . . . a . . . THOUSAND . . . GOLD . . . PIECES.

Servant That is a lot of money.

King Then these weavers must have a lot of money.
I must have the clothes at once.

Servant Very well, your Majesty. Here is the money, weavers. But remember, you heard the King say that he must have the clothes at once.

First Weaver That is easy. When we weave we have a magic touch. The cloth can be ready and the clothes made in just a few minutes.

Second Weaver You see, we have a magic touch, your Majesty.

King Then get to work.
I want the clothes.

First Weaver   We will go behind that screen and prepare the clothes. Then the King can put them on.

Second Weaver   Yes, your Majesty.
You must put them on.

Servant   Get ready to put on the clothes, your Majesty.

King   Very well. I will get ready.

Servant   You will soon have a fine suit of new clothes, your Majesty. And remember, you will also be able to find out who is clever and who is stupid.

King Yes, I shall soon know who is stupid . . .
AND . . . I shall soon find out who is not fit
to do his job.

Servant It will be most interesting, your Majesty.
Let me take your crown and your robes . . .
There! You are ready.

King Call the weavers.

Servant Weavers! Weavers! The King is ready.
Come forward and show the clothes.

First Weaver Here they are, your Majesty. See, we have
made you a magnificent suit of clothes with
our magic touch – trousers, coat and cloak.

Second Weaver Put them on, your Majesty.

King Well . . . Er . . . Yes . . . I cannot . . .

Servant I can see that the clothes really are
magnificent. Of course, that shows that I am
fit to do my job. Let me help you to put on the
beautiful trousers, your Majesty.

King I cannot . . .

First Weaver	Of course you can! The trousers fit perfectly.
Second Weaver	Put the coat on, your Majesty.
Servant	Yes, the coat is a perfect fit too. Now put on the cloak. I can see that everything fits perfectly.
King	I cannot . . .
First Weaver	Of course you can! Your new suit fits perfectly.

Servant Come, let us go out into the courtyard, so that all the people can see you. And remember! If people CAN'T SEE that you look magnificent, it is because they are not fit to do their jobs.

King Very well. I will come . . .
But . . .

First Weaver Stand forward, your Majesty, so that all may see.

Second Weaver Let everyone see you.

King But they are all . . .
They are all . . .

Servant LAUGHING! THEY ARE LAUGHING! ★

King Why are they laughing?

Servant They are laughing because they are stupid. They are calling out the most stupid remarks.

King What are they calling out?

Servant Well . . . They are saying . . . that . . . YOU HAVE NOTHING ON BUT YOUR VEST. But, don't worry, your Majesty. *I* can see the clothes.

King I don't believe you! I just don't believe you! Where are those weavers?

Servant They've gone!

King Bring them back! Bring them back! Those weavers have tricked me. They've tricked me. I HAVE NOTHING ON BUT MY VEST!

But by then the weavers had disappeared from sight with their pockets full of gold.

Things for you to do

1 ⟨c⟩o a t ends with ⟩o a t .

Use these letters and write more words which end with ⟩o a t .

⟨b⟩   ⟨g⟩   ⟨m⟩   ⟨st⟩   ⟨fl⟩

2 Write each sentence with the right word from the story.

(a) The castle door was opened by the King's (servant/master).

(b) The weavers said that they had a magic (wand/touch).

(c) The King loved beautiful (clothes/flowers).

(d) The weavers said that they must be paid a (hundred/thousand) gold pieces before they could begin to work.

3 Write these sentences in the right order for the story.

Then he took the invisible cloak.
First the King took the invisible trousers.
Next he took the invisible coat.

4 This is the Second Weaver saying one of the lines from his part.

I don't think we can do it.

Who said these lines?

(a) Just leave the thinking to me and say what I say.
(b) I must have the clothes at once.
(c) LAUGHING! THEY ARE LAUGHING!